SEASONS OF CHANGE

By: Regina Lynn Moses

ISBN: 978-1-960179-28-9

Cover Designs by: Chris Kitt Jr.

To contact author for booking or ordering
additional copies, go to:

regina_rome@yahoo.com

Table of Contents

Dedication

Acknowledgements

Introduction

Season of Deception

Season of Divorce

Season of Fear

Season of "What ifs"

Season of Mistaken Identity

Season of Finding Myself

A season of deception, divorce, fear, what if's, mistaken identity, and finding myself.

Dedication

To everyone who has had to survive struggles, hardship, relationships, hurt, or disappointment or even self-destruction; I am here to remind you that, while you may feel like things are impossible, even in your season of struggle, loneliness, or brokenness, with God, you can feel whole, restored, and renewed. You can survive whatever season you are going through. You are surviving.

Acknowledgements

To my Heavenly Father, who gives me the strength to wake up every morning and teaches me each day to manage every trial and blessing that comes my way. Thank you for teaching me how to survive this thing called life, to always lean on and depend on You and Your Word. I truly do not know where I would be without You, Heavenly Father, by my side, keeping me on this journey.

To my parents, who taught and showed me what it truly means to survive in life, in relationships, and in struggles: thank you for always being an example and for always being there. Thank you for always being my cheerleader, no matter what. Not everyone can say that, but I am glad that I can. Thank you for loving me, Mom and Dad.

Uncle Melvin, you have always been a quiet, soft-spoken man who stands like a giant. Thank you for always being there, doing for us without us even asking, for giving and helping out even when you didn't have to. Thank you for being that rock in my life!

To my loving son, DeAntione Rome: thank you for allowing me to guide us through this journey called survival and through the difficult seasons of change in our lives. Thank you for always loving me; having you in my life made me a better mom and person. You and God were the only things that kept me going and moving forward. I pray that I continue to make you proud of me. I love you more than life.

To my Godmother, Carol Wood: I want to say thank you for always being sensitive and obedient to the Spirit of God. I never would have thought of, or even imagined, drafting a book without your encouragement. I love and appreciate you more than you will ever know.

I would also like to thank the late Apostle Gus Kilgore, Jr., and First Lady Joann Kilgore for your guidance, love, and constant support during these seasons of my life. Thank you for not letting me stay stuck in my hurt, disappointment, and emotions. I love and miss you, Uncle Gus, and I appreciate you so much, Aunt Joann, for standing by my side.

I would like to acknowledge my pastors, Apostle Travis Jennings and Pastor Stephanie Jennings, for pushing me to not settle for being average. You motivate and encourage us to reach our potential, teaching me not to let my circumstances define what God has planned for my life.

Lastly, I want to express my appreciation to Amey, Joshua, and Merritt for supporting me on this journey to a place where I finally feel like I can survive anything. Thank you for being in my corner and for having my back.

Introduction

I cannot tell you how many times I struggled with beginning or drafting this book. I almost didn't, but I thank God for my godmother and my family, who encouraged me to share my story for my own healing and to help others who may have similar struggles. I want you to know that, even in the darkest seasons, when life feels hopeless and confusing, you can survive.

We must remember that our Heavenly Father is always with us, even in trials, storms, and seasons of decision-making. Our circumstances do not define who we are, regardless of what others may think. I want to share my journey, a story of heartbreak, the loss of a marriage, and grieving for a life I had envisioned with someone I thought would always be there. I've moved from a season of betrayal I feared would never end to a season of healing, of finding myself again, and of feeling whole. Yes, I am surviving. I am a survivor.

This was never the life I planned. If I'm honest, I never imagined I would be divorced and raising my son alone. I don't think anyone enters marriage expecting it to end, especially when they believe in their vows. We had been married for 13 years and talked about growing old together no matter what. But that wasn't how things unfolded. The thought of being single and having to make it work for my son and myself felt overwhelming. I was unprepared for what life was about to throw my way.

Growing up, my parents taught me to face life with honesty, trust my instincts, and treat others the way I wanted to be treated. They taught me the importance of forgiveness, making the best of every situation, and maintaining my character because, as they said, "your name is all you have." I am grateful for parents who believed in God and took us to church, where I learned to form my own relationship with my Lord and Savior, Jesus Christ. Little did I know that these lessons would be my foundation in surviving the unexpected shifts in my life.

As a child raised in the church, I learned many valuable lessons, but topics like mental health, abuse, and divorce were rarely discussed; they were taboo, especially in the context of marriage and family. I was encouraged to "pray and fast" over my struggles and not to share personal issues with others. While I don't believe my parents or church members were wrong, I do feel these subjects could have been discussed more openly, particularly around seeking counseling or support when relationships break down. At that time, I felt lost and alone, as though I had no one I could trust or talk to.

Surviving can feel relentless, like an elephant fending off a pack of lions. You keep running, trying to escape and return to normal life. That is exactly how I felt during these seasons, as if I were fighting just to stay above water, avoiding drowning in my own pain. I'm sure many can relate to feeling helpless and alone, not knowing where to turn or how to fix it. The one thing I believed to be secure, our marriage, was thrown away, leaving me in anguish from betrayal. The lies and the affair shattered my reality, and I found myself doubting my faith, my beliefs, and even God.

I wrestled with my emotions, feeling abandoned and angry. Blaming myself, thinking I had somehow caused it. Piecing my life back together, yet the real answer lay beyond my understanding.

As Isaiah 55:8 says: "For my thoughts are not your thoughts, neither are your ways my ways, declares the Lord."

At the time, I didn't fully grasp that God's love could heal my sorrow, heartache, hurt, pain, disappointment, and trust issues. I thought my situation was too big, too broken. Even though I knew of God's love, I couldn't feel it. My emotions clouded my vision, and I was dealing with a season of betrayal, fear, depression, and a sense of failure. But these shifting seasons were part of a necessary journey; one that I had to experience to reach where I am today.

Season of Deception

On December 23, he (my ex-husband) received a text message: *"We miss you and wish you were here to spend Christmas with us."* Initially, I thought it was family, but a second look at the message made me pause. I asked who it was from, and he brushed it off as nothing, so I let it go.

A few weeks later, I had a strange dream about kissing someone; it didn't feel true, but I took it as a warning to be careful. My grandmother "Big Mama" would teach us how to interpret our dreams, but I ignored the need to. Blinded by the love I had for him; I overlooked my discernment and instinct. If I had used Big Momma's teachings of the dream, I would have realized that it was him and that something deeper was at play. At least that's what I told myself, not knowing this would push me into a season of deception, four months later. All because I had chosen to continue to not push the envelope and trust him.

The day that changed my life, when I was chaperoning the prom for my school.

He was attentive, laughing, and holding conversation with all of us. At some point during the prom, he disappeared, and I found him asleep in the hotel lounge. I assumed he was tired from work. Not thinking much of it, I decided to take him home so that he could rest. When we arrived home, he stated that he needed to "go out" and promised he would be back soon. He did not return until early the next morning. When I confronted him, he was hesitant, but then admitted there was someone else. I paused in a moment of disbelief and then replied, 'Am I supposed to just walk away or panic because there is someone else?'

Inside, I was devastated, angry, hurt, and in disbelief, wondering how he could do this to me... to us. He sat there, looking afraid and scared, because usually I would have acted a fool. But my response to him was, 'I am not letting you go just because there is someone else.' At that moment, I was trying to be the woman that my momma, Big Momma, and God wanted me to be. I never imagined that I would have to deal with infidelity from my husband. I thought that we would always be together and grow old, but little did I know that our marriage would take a turn for the worse.

After a night out together, we talked about our future and decided to work on our marriage. I soon learned that the "other woman" was a co-worker of my husband. She was also well known by my father, brother-in law and many of our church members. The total disrespect and disregard for me and my family had reached a point where he did not care what anyone thought. Those who attended church with me knew about the affair and the situation between us, as some of them were friends with the "other woman". Can you imagine the betrayal I felt towards some of the church members? I was singing and laughing with them, unaware that they knew of the infidelities my husband and this "other woman" were engaging in. I talk to them all the time, yet no one said anything! After looking back, it felt like something right out of a movie.

I thank God that even in the middle of my brokenness, feeling alone, distraught, and utterly shattered I was able to give Him praise, to lift Him up. It was the only way I knew to find release and reassurance, to relieve the burden weighing on me. Church became my sanctuary, my refuge. What hurt me most, I think, was realizing that people in the congregation likely knew about his infidelity but said nothing or maybe it was that he clearly didn't care about me, doing whatever he pleased regardless. And then there was my father, trying to tell me the truth in ways he couldn't quite express; he wanted to protect me from the hurt. Yet, despite everything, I kept hoping, believing that God would somehow bring us back together.

Over time, I found receipts for things like children's clothes and toys that weren't for our son, along with other personal items that didn't belong in our home. The final blow came when he told me he was working, only for me to discover he'd been out of town with her. I felt betrayed and deceived. When he returned, I took our son and retreated to a friend's cabin to think, cry, pray, and decide what to do. I left without a clear plan, drowning in confusion, anger, and self-doubt. One moment, I felt hopeful; the next, I was angry with God, blaming myself for allowing it all to happen.

To cope, I started going to the park daily. While my son rode his bike, I walked, lost in thought, tears spilling over as I tried to keep my composure. Around him, I wore a brave face, though inside, I felt embarrassed and ashamed; ashamed of having failed at something I thought would last forever, just as my parents' 44-year marriage had. I believed that we would be doing the same.

Eventually, I felt I was healing or so I thought. We moved to another city, and I believed things were improving. But once he moved us, he left. Here I was, thinking we'd turned a corner, but he hadn't even had the courage to say, "I don't want this anymore." He just walked away as if it were nothing. My son was heartbroken, asking repeatedly why his daddy was leaving, where he was going, and I couldn't bring myself to tell him the truth.

I managed to handle the bills on my own, but things grew tight. I applied for a title loan for extra cash, choosing not to ask my family for help because I felt it was my responsibility to take care of us. I struggled, confused as to why God would allow this especially when I'd given Him my heart and my faith. I became desperate, reaching out to ministers and praying constantly, believing somehow that God would fix everything. I even turned to books like *A Praying Wife and A Praying Husband,* hoping the scriptures would restore my marriage. In the books, you could quote a scripture for your husband or wife. But as the distance between us grew, I started to feel that God wasn't listening. I was mad at God. I lost faith, was angry and disappointed, feeling abandoned. Due to the betrayal and deception in my marriage, I began to feel desperate. I needed to survive!

Depression began to settle in, and I struggled to find my footing, overwhelmed and drowning in despair. I felt like a failure. Surviving felt like swimming too far out to sea, where exhaustion sets in, and staying afloat becomes a losing battle. At that moment in my life these were my exact feelings, I was drowning! And yet, through the fear, brokenness, and uncertainty, I knew I had to trust in God, believing that He would see me through. Yes, God is my number one covering, but when you are married, you come together as one. He is also your covering as the head of the home, he's supposed to protect you, just as our Heavenly father protects and loves us. Sometimes, to survive, you will have to have faith in the things that are in front of you whether it's fear, brokenness, uncertainty, or being vulnerable to circumstances beyond your control. It's not easy; it's hard; extremely hard. We must put our trust in God and know, without any doubt, that God will see us through these circumstances. He knows our path better than we do!

Deception can make you believe everything that anyone says. It can make you gullible, preventing you from seeing the truth that is right in front of you. It blinds you to all the lies and games going on in the relationship, and sometimes, it desensitizes you. I must be real about this thing called deception: it doesn't only involve him at that time, but me as well. You might be wondering why I would say that. It's because I didn't allow myself to look at things for what they really were between us. I couldn't see what was happening, trying to prove that what my heart, mind, and my eyes were seeing was wrong. At that time, I thought I wasn't enough for him, even though I knew God. But in that moment, I forgot who God was in my life. I was caught up in all the anger, pain, and distrust in my marriage. By not remembering that God was enough for me and my son, I let what I couldn't see cloud my judgment, trying to be the woman that I thought my parents and others expected me to be.

Due to all the stress from finding out about the affair, along with him pretending to be at work while spending time with her in and out of town, I was at my breaking point. What pushed me over the edge was that he hadn't stopped seeing and dealing with her, despite promising that we would work things out. I thought I was managing everything, but I wasn't. One morning, I woke up to find the left side of my face swollen, along with the left side of my body. I was admitted to the hospital for a couple of days.

The fear of losing everything and not being able to properly deal with things led me to that point. A friend of mine who worked at the hospital said, "Regina, you cannot let this get the best of you. You have a son to think about, and if you do not get it together, he won't have a mother, and you do not want someone else taking care of him." My life would have been a little different if I hadn't allowed myself to continue to take everything the wrong way. I had to change my priorities, which meant putting my son and myself first. But changing how I handled things wasn't easy, it never is. I knew then I had to do this, and that's when fear and uncertainty began to show up in my life. I could tell that this next season would bring an uncomfortable shift.

Season of Divorce

One day, while I was working in my classroom, I received a call from the front office asking me to come up. As I was walking to the front office, I was wondering what it could be about. I knew I hadn't done anything wrong, at least nothing I could think of. When I arrived at the front office, two police officers were waiting for me. The closer I got to them, the more my thoughts raced. I couldn't believe they could be here for me. I started to pray that nothing was wrong with my son or my parents.

As I entered the front office, one of the officers approached me and said, "I have something for you." I looked at him, confused, and took the paper he handed me. My heart started pounding. "You've been served," he said. I asked him what it was, and then realized it was divorce papers being handed to me right in front of my co-workers. I couldn't even look at them after the officer gave them to me. I walked out of the front office as though nothing had happened. I was hurt, embarrassed, disappointed and mad as h---. I kept thinking, "Who would do a low-down dirty thing like that to someone?" I was deeply disappointed in him for feeling like he had to do something like this. I thought our relationship was in a better place than that.

Yes, we were separated, but I have always carried myself as an approachable person, at least that's how I thought of myself. I wasn't one to enjoy confrontation, because I knew that if I was pushed too far, no one would like the result. So, when God saved me, it changed me. If this had happened before God delivered me, I might have reacted differently. I could have understood him doing it that way if I had been that type of person. But the way he did it, that's what has puzzled me the most out of this situation. It made me feel as though I was the one causing all the problems and disruption. It showed me that I really didn't know him like I thought I did. On that day, I was so upset that I was numb, crying all the way back to my classroom.

There was already so much going on before I received those divorce papers. It felt like nothing I said or did was right, like it didn't matter to him. It made me feel like the little trust that remained between us was gone. I kept thinking to myself, "How dare he act like I was the one causing all the chaos, the one who cheated, the one who lied, when it was him." I reached a point where I realized he really didn't care how this was affecting me. It was like him threatening to take our son from me, like he thought I would cave. One thing's for sure, you truly never know a person until opposition arises.

You don't know how far they'll go or how dishonest they can be. But one thing I knew for certain: I wasn't going to give up my son to make things easier for him. Yes, I was stressed, upset, and disappointed by all of this, but I knew I had solid ground for not losing our son because of his infidelity. Hey, maybe I was naïve to think that he would play fair; to think he would do the right thing, especially considering he was in church and was supposed to be saved. But to try to make it seem like I was the unfit one in this marriage, that was the moment I realized I wasn't dealing with the same person that I married. He had become a stranger, no longer the person I had fallen in love with.

In this storm, I found myself repeatedly asking God, "Why? Why is he doing this?" I remember it clearly, like it happened yesterday. There was a movie by Tyler Perry called *Diary of a Mad Black Woman*. I didn't know much about the movie, but I knew it was from one of my favorite screenwriters. I remember sitting in the theater, watching scenes unfold that mirrored different moments of my life. It felt as though I was reliving everything all over again, and before I knew it, I was crying uncontrollably. I completely lost myself in that moment. The pain, the anguish, the hurt; all of it came flooding back. It felt like I was part of the movie, exposed for the whole world to see.

I left the movie theater thinking "WOW." I found myself begging, wanting God to fix it for me, but there was no answer. To be completely honest, I do not think I would have been able to hear him at that time, and it wasn't because God wasn't listening or speaking to me. It was because I was too busy trying to fix and solve the problems in my marriage on my own. I was feeling sorry for myself and wasn't patient enough to wait and hear from God about how to handle it. I was just trying to survive the blows, bumps, and turmoil in my life. This season was tough.

There was a court date for child support, but instead, it turned out to be about proceeding with the divorce. I wasn't expecting that at all. I was blindsided, again. I hadn't been looking at the bigger picture; I was still holding out hope that my marriage would eventually work out. When I arrived in court, the judge could immediately tell from the expression on my face that I was unaware of what was happening. He asked me if I knew about the proceedings, and I told him no. I thought it was supposed to be about child support. Reluctantly, I went along with the proceedings. You know how it is when you're trying to make things work whether it is for me or for him. I was trying to make sure that, despite everything that had happened, this was still the right decision for both of us. I even asked him if he was sure, and he paused as if he wasn't sure, but then said yes. In that moment, I realized I was fighting for someone who wasn't putting as much thought, energy, or love into this relationship or this marriage as I was.

On that day, my sister and my best friend stood by me. I wanted to do something out of the norm, something wild and unexpected, lolz. So, I asked her if she would take me to get a tattoo. I had always played it safe and playing it safe had led me to where I was that day. At least, that was what I thought at that time. I figured it was better than going out drinking, having sex, or being irresponsible. It felt like I had always done what everyone expected me to do. Yes, I was still saved, but it didn't stop me from feeling lost. Facing one of my worst fears of becoming a divorced parent was a harsh reality. In my family, my parents, auntie, uncles, and even grandparents had been married for a long time. That's what I wanted, not a divorce.

I decided to do something that would provide a temporary fix. Feeling anxious, desperate, and suffering from panic attacks; I found myself in a season of fear and uncertainty. Even after the court decision regarding the divorce, I thought that he would come back. I would still be intimate with him, knowing that he was with her. I felt guilty, knowing that after being with me, he would return to her. Finally, I decided enough was enough. I told him I could no longer live this way, allowing him to come and go as he pleased. That was one of the hardest decisions I have ever made; putting trust in God, believing He would keep me spiritually and physically strong. I had to learn to depend on God for everything.

I felt like I put him before God, not realizing that's exactly what I was doing. Yes, I allowed myself to get involved with him intimately, but I thought I was doing what was right and best for me. However, it was not God's plan for my life. Even though I knew God, stood on His word, and believed in His promises, that didn't prevent the situation from happening. Nor did it stop the enemy from attacking my mind, thoughts, feelings, and spirit.

It presented opposition that I wasn't prepared for.

If you had asked me how I was feeling at that time, I would have said strong, determined, funny, confident, independent, loving, and caring. I knew who I was as a wife, a Christian, and a child of God. Nothing could shake my faith, and I believed I could handle anything. I felt ready for opposition, knowing I would bounce back and continue to lean on God. But that's when everything started to unravel; misunderstanding, disagreements, miscommunication, lies, and chaos. We could have worked things out, and become good co-parenting partners, but the insecurity of the other woman prevented that. It felt like I had failed God all over again.

During the separation and divorce, I went through financial hardship. I am a prideful person, but I needed help from him. My income was not enough to cover our essential needs, and I didn't have money for food. A coworker gave me $5 at that time. The Burger King had Happy Meals on sale for $0.99, so after basketball practice, I stopped and bought two Happy Meals for us. I did whatever I could to make ends meet, especially when things were tight. I would scrape together the money just to ensure we had food to eat. I even struggled to have enough gas to get to work or the grocery store.

I decided to call my son's father to see if he could help us, even just a little. His response was, "If you wouldn't spend the money that I send you for child support on yourself, you'd have money." I told him I use the money to pay for bills, utilities, and things we needed. I don't use it on myself. His response made me so angry and upset that I vowed never to ask for anything again. If he truly cared for his son, no matter how he felt about me, he would help financially without making it a problem. I knew it would be hard and rough at times, but I had hoped he would want to be there for our son. I regretted asking him for help, but I chose to put aside my pride and asked anyway.

I told God, "I don't know how I'm going to make it, but I need your help. I can't do this on my own." Then, the devil began to attack my thoughts. I felt like God failed me, but it wasn't God, it was him. I had started leaning on my own understanding of how to fix my marriage, how it should work, and how things needed to unfold in our relationship. I was trying to take control of the situation, believing that was the way God wanted things to go. But I wasn't making anything better.

In the word of God (Proverbs 3: 5-6) says:

"Trust in the Lord with all thine heart; lean not your own understanding. In all of thy ways acknowledge him, and he shall direct thy path."

I wanted all of that, but the part that says, "In all of thy ways acknowledge" was hard for me to admit. It's difficult to admit that my way wasn't working. All the screaming, crying, fussing, pouting, anger, and hurt hadn't changed a thing. It was hard to let go of control and submit to defeat.

I had to acknowledge and admit to God that my way was not working:

"I give up if you do not help me. I don't think that I can make it. I don't think I will survive this."

God was saying even though things are shattered, and things aren't going the way you want, let Me direct your path. This means that, even if everything I thought was important doesn't turn out the way I desire, I must "acknowledge" it. I had to tell myself that this part of my season was over.

I am surviving, I am a savior, even though it may not seem like it, and it may not look or feel like a victory. This season, I did not win.

Season of Fear

I want to talk a little bit about the spirit of fear. It can come in many forms and disguises. Fear is defined as an unpleasant emotion or belief that someone or something is dangerous, often caused by pain or threat, which can lead to self-protection. However, fear can also hold you hostage and paralyze you. How many know that the spirit of fear can, at times, kill dreams, destroy relationships, and stop you from acting out or responding?

You know, I used to be afraid of arguing or getting into disagreement with my ex-husband because I didn't want things to get out of hand. I knew how my temper had been in the past, and I didn't know how to argue in a healthy way. My behavior came from what I had seen and experienced, and the effects it had. So, I decided not to allow myself to get into situations where I'd feel backed up in a corner and compelled to say something I couldn't take back. I hated the feeling of helplessness after everything was over. The spirit of fear kept me from speaking up for myself at times. Back then, I would be quiet because I didn't know how to communicate my feelings. I was still trying to be the bigger person in the situation.

You know, black women are often labeled as angry, mad, or vindictive. I was supposed to be different, especially being raised the way I was being saved. I didn't know it was okay to sometimes be uncomfortable with being uncomfortable. Fear can also hinder decision- making, especially in important areas in your life. For me, I often operated out of fear; the fear of loneliness, the fear of not being enough, and the fear of failure.

You know, before I got married, I was already dealing with the fear of loneliness. Even before I ever met my ex-husband, I wrestled with the thought and the fear of always being by myself, never falling in love, or never getting married or having children. Fear also interferes with your confidence; it makes you second-guess things that have been solid and stable in your life. So, when I met him, I thought that I had beaten the spirit of fear and loneliness.

But little did I know, it was still there, just hiding. Fear also stemmed from my own insecurity of abandonment. It showed up when I started going through my seasons of lies, betrayal and divorce. When I began to recognize it all, I realized my biggest fear had come true; being alone, having someone walk away from us, and not having anyone to love us. I kept thinking, "Is this really happening?"

You know, if you don't do anything about it, the spirit of fear will always wreak havoc in your life. It will always be a constant reminder of "What if?" You don't want to be continually taunted by the spirit of fear. To survive a season, you have to face the things that are in front of you. The spirit of fear can trigger anxiety, insecurity, depression, loneliness, and failure. For me, it was hard to shake off, and it was difficult to stand on the Word of God because I was fearful of how I might respond to the situation I was facing. At times, I would stand on my faith and belief in God and His Word, but sometimes I didn't, due to the fear of anxiety, the emotions of failure, and my insecurity even though it wasn't seen. I also struggled with the thought of church members knowing about my situation and judging me. I knew people were watching and expecting me to carry myself in a certain way. I knew some wanted me to act the fool, and believe me, at times I wanted to, and I did. But I knew that wasn't the way God wanted me to act.

Fear had me in a bad space. It made me feel disconnected from myself, my family, and God. The feeling of disconnect came from the threat of losing everything I couldn't fully grasp. It was the disconnect from what used to be sound and dependable in my life, leaving me feeling empty and like I wasn't even existing. It's a disconnection from God, a relationship that relocates us to a place we're unfamiliar with. Fear puts you in a very dark and distant place. It made me distant from everyone and everything. Fear can stifle and halt whatever you were doing; deferring any plans God has for you without you even realizing it. Guess what? Fear doesn't want you, or me, to admit that we're scared, and it doesn't want us to talk about it. It doesn't want me to admit how fearful I was about walking

through this season of my life; going from
dealing with someone I thought was the one,
to having no one. From having security to
having none. From being stable to unstable.
Walking in fear made me constantly depend
on things falling through for me, always
thinking I would fail at everything I wanted
or needed to do. It made me think that fear
was waiting for me just around the corner.

Fear is that distraction that keeps you
in a space far away from victory God has
intended for you. It prevents us from
stepping into God's plan and hinders us from
completing the purpose He has set for us on
this earth.

In Psalm 23:4 it says, "Even though I walk
through the darkest valley, I will fear no
evil, for you are with me; your rod and your
staff, they comfort me."

Yes, what I was going through felt
like death. I lost him, and it truly felt like a
form of death, but was different. When
someone dies, you no longer see them or
talk to them. But with him, and with the
situation, it was dead to me, while he was
still alive. It takes time in prayer and

meditation on God and His Word to defeat fear. I had to stop allowing the spirit of fear to have its way in my life. I had to give it to God; my doubts, my fears, my deepest feelings, and relinquish all the control I thought I had. I am not saying that it was easy.

It wasn't. I had built up so many negative thoughts, and the fear of abandonment that I clung to while dealing with everything was difficult to release. I had to allow God to tear down everything in my life and rebuild me, to heal me mentally, physically, and spiritually, so I could be where He wanted me to be in that season. This battle taught me how to fight, how to stand strong in my faith, and to trust that no matter how hard or how difficult it may get, I should not fear what I may see or hear. I had to know that no matter how impossible things seemed, I could SURVIVE. And so can you.

Surviving this has taught me resilience. It taught me how to fight, how to stand strong in my faith in God, and how not to let my fears overtake me and wreak havoc. Because there were times when I didn't want to be bothered by anyone. All I wanted to do was sleep due to the depression, wallowing in my pity and being left alone. There were times when I cried and I mean, I cried a lot. During those moments, I closed myself off and shut down. I was deeply depressed. I'd come home from work, acting as though everything was fine, but deep down, I was emotionally drained from it all. I would go into my room, close the door, and break down in tears, hoping my son wouldn't hear me.

Some days, it feels like the impossible just keeps piling up, and it can seem as though all hope is lost. But even in those moments, it's vital to spend time in prayer and meditation. The strength of God is profound, far greater than any hopelessness we could ever experience. He does not want us to fear, even when we can't see the solution to our most pressing problems. If we remain in Him, God will be there, extending His mighty hand to guide and sustain us.

Deuteronomy *31:6* reminds us: "The Lord himself goes before you and will be with you; he will never leave you nor forsake you. Do not be afraid; do not be discouraged."

This scripture has shown me how to stand firm and not allow fear to overtake me. And if fear tries to return, I now have a solid foundation on which to stand and fight. The foundation is in God; a foundation that cannot be moved. For God has not given us the spirit of fear but of power, love, and a sound mind to face whatever comes my way.

Season of "What If"

There was a season of "What if…"

My season of "What if" came with more questions than answers. Do you know what it's like to have a bunch of "what if" questions flooding your mind? *What if I had handled situations differently? What if I had lost some weight?* These thoughts consumed me, especially because of the other woman. They attacked my self-esteem, confidence, and body image.

She was smaller than me at the time, and I carried more weight than I wanted to wearing sizes 22 to 26 while she might have been 14 to 16. My mind spiraled with questions like, what if I lost more weight? What if I got the liposuction I had always dreamed of? Would he come back to me? Would it be enough then? I began to wonder if fixing my appearance and eliminating my imperfections would change everything.

I even questioned whether I had loved him enough or been attentive to his needs. The lies he was fed, like "She doesn't care about you" or "She doesn't want you to look good," left me second guessing myself. I had always made sure he knew he was loved; I told him often, encouraged him, and ensured he looked his best. How could he believe otherwise? I blamed myself for his betrayal. My "What ifs" became endless loops as I tried to justify his actions. I asked God for answers, but didn't quiet myself long enough to hear His response. Looking back now, I see it clearly: it wouldn't have mattered what I did. He still would have cheated.

But the "What ifs" didn't stop. They whispered lies into my thoughts, pulling me toward anger and negativity. There was even a moment when I thought, *What if I just ended it all for both of them?* I planned to confront them with a gun, but it mysteriously went missing before I could act. That missing gun was God's protection.

When I look back at what went down it would not have mattered what I had done he still would have cheated and been unfaithful. My what if that I thought was over, but it was not it was still there whispering in my ear, my thoughts, and my mind. It started to take me toward an extremely negative and evil place. My what if during this season went to what if you just went and shot the them both? Hey, you are supposed to be the dumb one they played you, so just get the gun. When I did decide to do it, the gun was missing. He had just purchased a gun about months before all of this.

I also thought, *"What if I showed up at their job, acted a plum fool, and made a scene?"* I wanted to act out, to make them feel the pain I was experiencing. But deep down, I knew it wouldn't accomplish anything. It wouldn't bring him back, and it certainly wasn't the way God wanted me to respond.

The enemy filled my mind with lies: *What if no one ever loves you again? What if you're always alone? What if no man wants a divorced woman with a child?* It was a battle of the mind; a fight I wasn't prepared for, in this season.

During this season, I found myself going to church more than ever. The church became my refuge, my place of peace amidst the storm. I read the Bible, prayed, and leaned on God. I began to realize that "What if" was a distraction, one that kept me trapped in my emotions and away from God's truth. I needed God to heal my pain, hurt, the hatred that I was feeling.

At times, if you are not careful, you may find yourself stressing over every little thing, trying anything to answer all of the questions of "what if." One thing that I have learned is there will always be a "what if" in your life." It's how you manage it when it comes that truly matters.

I have also learned that, during the different seasons of life, no matter what is happening, some outcomes are beyond your control. It doesn't matter if you scream, fast, pray, pout, or even have unshakable faith in God, there are times when you must let go and accept whatever way things unfold, trusting that our Heavenly Father has our best interests at heart.

Sometimes, what is best or good for us hurts. It may even cause you to second-guess God's plan for your life. It may stress you out or test your faith and beliefs. But we must remember we are surviving, and I am a survivor.

I had to learn how to navigate the highs and lows of my season, as well as the desert-like situations in my life. To help myself survive and escape the cycle of bad thoughts and fear of failure, I started focusing more on my son and the blessings right in front of me.

Healing did not come easy for me. I pretended everything was fine, acting like nothing was wrong or happening. I walked with my head high and my chest out, as if it were just another normal day. But inside, all I wanted was for God to heal me from the pain I was feeling.

Do not get me wrong, there's nothing wrong with walking around confidently, hiding your pain. But it's crucial not to get caught up in appearances that you don't allow God to heal you. Healing requires an open heart, and it happens in His time, not ours. I wanted and needed God to work on me immediately, but I had to wait.

To survive this season of my life, I made it my responsibility to ensure my son was okay mentally and spiritually. I worked to shield him from the harsh realities of what was happening, especially from church members who knew about his father leaving us and moving in with the other woman. These same members had children who were friends with our son, making it more challenging.

It was important to me that he didn't feel abandoned, unloved, or unwanted. Focusing on my son and his well-being helped me push forward.

They say that the church is your hospital; a place where you can find whatever you need: healing, deliverance, joy, and love. For me, the church became my hospital. God became my doctor, lawyer, deliverer, and healer. Growing up, God was always my strength, and even in this season, I could not stop leaning on Him.

I threw myself into ministry, working with the youth and participating in everything the church was offering. I thank

God for a praying pastor and first lady who encouraged me and pushed me through the storm. Their guidance helped me heal.

The more I threw myself into church and ministry, the stronger I felt. Gradually, I reached a point where hearing their names or seeing them together no longer made me angry or sick to my stomach. I no longer held animosity or hatred toward them, even knowing I might never receive an apology.

Through it all, I discovered that God is a healer and a restorer. He restored my heart, my mind, my soul, and my spirit. Today, I can say with confidence: I am a survivor, and I am Surviving this season.

Season of Mistaken Identity

Life has a way of throwing the unexpected at you, but nothing could have prepared me for the season of mistaken identity that turned my world upside down. While I was already dealing with the aftermath of a court proceeding, I suddenly found myself entangled in a nightmare I never saw coming.

One morning, as I was heading out to take my son to school and then go to work, I was stopped by the police. I pulled over and waited for the officer to approach my car. He asked for my license and registration, the usual routine. However, after a long wait, another police vehicle pulled up. Both officers approached me and asked if I could step out of the car. Confused and nervous, I complied.

As we walked toward the back of my car, my mind raced. When we stopped, one of the officers began questioning me. "Do you go by any name other than Regina?" he asked. "No," I responded firmly. "Do you have any visible tattoos?" "Yes," I replied, explaining that I had tattoos on my right shoulder and hip. Then, he dropped the bombshell: they were taking me in.

Stunned, I asked, "Are you really going to arrest me in front of my son?" My heart broke at the thought of him watching his mother being taken away. The officer assured me that my son would not see me handcuffed and arranged for another officer to take him to school. As I watched my son drive away, his little face pressed against the window, filled with fear and uncertainty, I felt helpless.

I was taken to Rockdale County Jail, and to my shock, I ran into a student from the school where I worked. The embarrassment of seeing a familiar face in such a setting was overwhelming. After spending a day in Rockdale, I was transported to Gwinnett County Jail, where the situation worsened.

They fingerprinted me and demanded that I sign paperwork identifying myself as Victoria Sturgis. "I am not Victoria Sturgis," I insisted. "My name is Regina Lynn Rome. I will not sign anything claiming otherwise."

Despite my protests, I was treated as if I were someone else. I went through the full intake process; stripped, showered with disinfectant, and handed an orange jumpsuit. The humiliation and disbelief were unbearable. I shared a cell with two other women, but sleep was impossible. After they put me in the room with them, I was still thinking this really must be a bad dream. And right now, was it something that I said was it something that I did was it a cruel joke that's what I was really thinking. And as I waited to hear from my family about what was going on there was still nothing that they could actually tell me at that time.

And on that third night of being there I realized that I probably wouldn't be able to come home, I probably would never see my son again or my family. And here I was before this happened worrying about the things that my husband did before all of this happened. How my world felt like it was torn apart, it was no longer important. I went to bed that night. I started to cry and one of the inmates whispered it's going to be alright I cried myself to sleep that night. I tried my best to be strong but all I could think of was people go to jail all the time for things that they didn't do, and they are never able to prove that it wasn't them.

I got a chance to call one of my closest friends who coaches at the school with me. I told him about what was going on with me. I asked him to keep it between us, which he did; I would call him when I needed assurance. I began to get concerned and started praying that I don't lose my job while I'm in jail.

While I was waiting to hear back from the attorney and my sister. My job was in jeopardy and the principal said that she could only give me to that Friday and if I wasn't I no longer had a job. My thoughts were what am I'm going to do I was missing my son; I found myself praying. I had started to think that I was not going to ever get out or not knowing that my sister and family were working hard behind the scenes to get me out.

After three days, I was taken to court. The judge addressed me as Victoria Sturgis, but I refused to accept that name. "I am not her," I stated, my voice unwavering. My sister stood up and confirmed that I had legal representation. The judge seemed surprised but unconcerned.

I spent five more days in jail before my sister was able to prove my innocence. Victoria had been writing fraudulent checks, purchasing cars in my name, and committing financial crimes across multiple counties.

I was transferred from Gwinnett County to Forsyth County jail after I got there. I can remember one officer saying when they brought me in. Is she the one from Gwinnett County? And they said yes, she told them don't put her in that cell. They have her all over the news and they're saying that we arrested the wrong person, and the sheriff doesn't want the news media outside the facility. She said that it was identity theft and that she is not the one. That it's a mistaken identity. They released me later that night where I met my sister and niece along with the news media.

The injustice of it all was crushing. Even after my release, the experience haunted me. Every time I got behind the wheel, I checked my rearview mirror, afraid that at any moment, I would be mistaken for her again.

Then, on Father's Day weekend, it happened again. I was at my sister's house, preparing food for our father, when police sirens filled the air. An officer knocked on the door and asked whose car was parked outside. I told them it was mine, and they asked me to step outside. "We have a warrant for your arrest from Bibb County," the officer announced.

I was taken to DeKalb County Jail and later transferred to Bibb County. This time, I knew what to expect, but it didn't make it any easier. During my time there, my cousins worked as one of the nurses on duty that day when I came in and the other was a fireman that was working there at the time when they brought me in. I broke done crying when I saw Donzella and Lonnie. I knew that God was letting me know that everything will be alright. That God had me and he has my back. Once again, my sister fought to clear my name, and after two and a half days, I was released.

By this point, I was emotionally drained. But this season was not over yet. The final incident occurred when I was pulled over again. The officer told me there was yet another warrant for my arrest. By then, I had no patience left. "I am not Victoria Sturgis!" I snapped. "She stole my identity!"

For the first time, an officer actually listened. He advised me to report my stolen identity officially and to carry a legal document proving my innocence. I followed his advice, and the authorities finally gave me a special identification pin to prevent future wrongful arrests.

This season of mistaken identity taught me invaluable lessons. I became more cautious, more aware of the company I kept, and more determined than ever to stand up for myself. The experience made me appreciate the power of faith.

Exodus 14:14 says, "The Lord will fight for you; you need only to be still." And through it all, I learned that no matter what season I face, I must remain steadfast and unshakable. Seasons change, and life shifts, but with faith and perseverance, I will always overcome.

Season of Finding Myself

I went through many seasons that almost cost me everything. I felt lost. When you go through a difficult season, it doesn't just affect you, but it impacts everyone connected to you. In finding myself, I emerged from a place of silence, discovering a voice through writing, talking, and having open conversations about my experiences. It gave me the opportunity to share what was happening in my life, to tell my story and speak the truth.

In the past, I would have taken so much from people without saying anything. But finding myself gave me a chance to correct the lies and misconceptions about me. I had remained silent because I didn't know how to fight without coming from a place of destruction or being perceived as a vengeful, spiteful, or bitter woman. That's often the label placed on us when we express anger or act out from the hurt others have caused.

During this journey of self-discovery, I had to admit that my divorce had taken everything out of me. I wasn't the same person I was before or even during my marriage. I decided it was time to leave the dark places I had been living in and let go of the brokenness so God could truly commune with me. With the help of God, we fought my battle. I learned to speak my mind without damaging or hurting anyone purposefully. I now speak and tell my truth unapologetically and with confidence, boldness and energetically.

I decided to deal with the pain, the hurt, and the sense of failure while finding the value of my strength and the importance of my support system. Prayers from others and the unwavering presence of faithful friends showed up unexpectedly when I needed them the most. Sometimes, we don't need advice, lectures, or opinions; we just need someone to listen.

One of my friends allowed me to cry and vent about everything I was going through. She let me have my pity party, but when she'd had enough, she firmly said, "Gurrrlll, you need to stop crying and get yourself together because, gurl, he has moved on." Her words were hard for me to hear, but they woke me up. I thank God for friends and a support system that didn't judge me, cast me away, or make me feel unworthy nor unwanted.

I thank God for cutting the emotional ties and desires I still had for my ex-husband. I had been in bondage, stuck in turmoil over something that could never be the same. Finding my true self again was a process; not something instant, like heating up something in the microwave. Rediscovering who I am and what I want took time.

During this process, I learned to accept and understand my feelings, relationships, thoughts, goals, and new dreams. I relearned and re-established what mattered to me, reconnecting with God in the process. Finding myself allowed me to align my values, passions, visions, and purposes that God has intended for my life.

Accepting my past was crucial for dealing with my present and working towards my future. Living authentically meant rewriting my life and embracing my unique story. I learned to trust again, relax, and exhale without panic, fear, or doubt. I began to trust myself and my judgment more as I moved forward, overcoming obstacles that once weighed me down.

You can easily lose your identity when burdened by life expectations, trauma, pain, or the need to please others. For a time, I gave more to others and less to myself. Growing up, I was taught the type of person I should be; confident, loving, caring, compassionate, and independent. Somewhere along the way, I forgot about those lessons,

I had to remind myself that my identity doesn't come from others. It comes from Christ. My father taught me practical skills like changing a tire, oil, and even an alternator, but I became dependent on my ex-husband to handle those things and forgot my own capabilities. I come from a legacy of proud, hardworking, talented women, and yet, I lost sight of who I was while trying to be the wife I thought my ex wanted.

My foundation; what God and my parents instilled in me had been buried under the weight of my relationship. But my identity is in Christ. I now seek Him for validation, confirmation, and affirmation, not people or circumstances.

I come from a royal priesthood. When God made me, He didn't make a mistake. "I Am Beautiful and Wonderfully Made." Even though my situation was ugly at the time, I've been reminded that God never makes mistakes.

On my journey of finding myself, I realized it was important to discover **who I am not.** I had to ask myself challenging questions I wasn't ready to face in the past. This process began with self-discovery or self-reflection or whatever you want to call it. I had to allow myself to embrace growth, heal, and truly change.

My godmother started this process by asking me some crucial questions that later helped shape this book. One question was, *"What has suppressing your feelings made you feel?"* My answer: weak, vulnerable, inadequate, incapable, silenced, unwanted, angry, anxious, and sometimes even depressed.

Another question was: *How did the dagger in your back make you feel?* I responded that it made me feel hurt, unappreciated, and damaged. It caused me to lose hope in myself and others and left me questioning people's motives. I no longer trusted at face value; instead, I second-guessed everyone and everything.

I learned the hard way, not everyone has your best interests at heart. Blindly trusting people often leads to betrayal. I became more cautious about who I allowed in my life. I felt unassured, irrelevant, and sometimes even useless, like no one really understood me. I often wondered if the dagger was my fault. Did I cause it through something I did or said? These feelings haunted me until I confronted them during my journey of self-reflection.

One particularly tough question was: *Who made you feel the most rejected?* My answer was painful but honest; church members, family, and even myself. I realized I had rejected myself due to my circumstances, including the failure of my marriage. This revelation, while difficult, was necessary for my healing.

I needed God to heal me, starting with my mind, then my heart, and finally restoring my faith, trust, and love. Without God, I would've been nothing more than an empty shell. I had to relearn and re-establish who I was.

I asked myself: *How would the real Regina describe herself?* The real Regina would say she's allowing God to piece back together the parts of her that were torn, broken, and ripped away. She's working to become the best version of herself, the person she was before the storm. Regina is healing, yet still cautious. She now questions people's motives, which she did not do before.

At times, this new awareness interferes with her judgment, daily decisions, and even her obedience to God. Yet, she sees hope, happiness, and love in her life, despite the enemy's attempt to destroy it. Regina is learning to trust God fully. He has mended her heart and healed her scars. She believes she will love again, and that God has prepared the perfect partner for her.

The Regina you see now will never allow her relationship with God to go dormant again. She's determined to keep moving forward with His help. When I look at myself, I see someone who has endured so much and yet remains standing as someone determined to make the best of life.

I've learned to channel my emotions and frustrations differently by relying entirely on God. This is something I had never fully done before. In the past, I would pick up my problems and try to fix them myself. Now, I love the person I am becoming. I'm doing what feels right for me, what aligns with my desires and God's plan rather than conforming to others' expectations.

These were just some of the questions I had to ask myself on this journey of rediscovery. This process was necessary for healing and moving forward. I began to declare to myself: *Who is in charge of your life, your circumstances, yourself, or God?*

When we feel anxious, we must relinquish control to God. This act of surrender allows us to refocus, redirect, and be refined. It gives God the opportunity to handle the problem or show us how to do so.

We must confront these hard questions if we want to be free, free from bondage, self-infliction, and self-judgment. Seasons come and go in life, and we must decide how to handle them. Will we let the season define us? Will we give up, or will we fight? Trust that God will take care of you, no matter the season or the shifts it brings.

I pray that everyone who reads this book finds healing in their current season, that they learn to embrace the shifts in their lives, and that our Savior, Jesus Christ, makes them whole even in the most difficult seasons.

www.ingramcontent.com/pod-product-compliance
Lightning Source LLC
Chambersburg PA
CBHW060143150626
46550CB00014B/1251

*9 7 8 1 9 6 0 1 7 9 2 7 2 *